KU-078-494

5. Cut the dough in half. Put half of it back into the fridge. Divide the rest into five pieces.

6. Put a little flour on your hands and squeeze and roll the dough into sausage shapes.

7. Gently flatten each shape then use a blunt knife to make four cuts for legs.

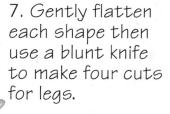

8. Gently pull the legs apart. Pinch their ends into points and bend them out.

9. Take the other half of the dough out of the fridge and make five more octopuses.

10. Lift the octopuses onto a baking tray. Bake them for 10-12 minutes.

11. Leave them to cool for a little while before putting them on a cooling rack.

12. Follow step 8 on page 21 to make icing. Put some icing on the sweets. Press them on for eyes.

Jam tarts

For about 12 tarts, you will need:
150g (6oz) plain flour
75g (3oz) margarine
6 teaspoons of very cold water
pinch of salt
jam
greased baking tray with shallow pans
round cutter
tiny cutters

Making pastry

To make the tarts

1. Mix the flour and the salt. Rub in the margarine so that it looks like crumbs.

2. Add the water. Use a blunt knife to mix it in. Squeeze it into a ball of dough.

3. Sprinkle flour onto your work surface. Roll out the dough thinly.

4. Press out 12 shapes from the dough with the round cutter.

If you haven't got any tiny cutters use a bottle top instead.

What shall I cook?

Contents

Before you start any of the recipes in this book, make sure that you have all the things you will need. Always ask someone to help you to switch on your oven to the correct temperature, before you begin to cook. Also ask for help when you put things into an oven or take things out of it. Wear a pair of oven gloves before you pick up anything which might be hot.

Chocolate octopuses

For 10 octopuses, you will need:
125g (4oz) soft margarine
125g (4oz) caster sugar
1 medium egg
3 tablespoons of cocoa powder
175g (6oz) plain flour
sweets for eyes
greased baking tray

For butter icing:
25g (1oz) butter
50g (2oz) icing sugar
lemon juice

1. Mix the sugar and margarine in a bowl with a wooden spoon until they are creamy.

2. Sift the flour and the cocoa into the bowl. Add the egg and mix them well to make dough.

3. Use your hands to press the dough into a large ball. Wrap it in plastic foodwrap.

4. Put the wrapped dough into a freezer for 30 minutes or into a fridge for an hour.

Heat the oven to gas mark 6, 200°C, 400°F

5. Push the shapes into a greased tin. Put a teaspoon of jam into each one.

6. Press out some shapes with the tiny cutters. Put one on each tart.

7. Bake the tarts for about 15 minutes in your oven.

8. Take care as the tarts will be very hot. Leave them to cool on a rack.

Wait until the tarts are cold to eat them.

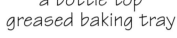

Cheesy snakes and caterpillars

For about eight snakes and four caterpillars, you will need:
150g (6oz) self-raising flour
½ teaspoon salt
25g (1oz) margarine
75g (3oz) cheese, finely grated
1 egg and 2 tablespoons of milk, beaten together
raisins for eyes
a bottle top
greased baking tray

1. Sift the flour and salt. Add the margarine and rub it with your fingers to make crumbs.

2. Leave a tablespoon of cheese on a saucer. Add the rest to the bowl and stir it in.

3. Put a tablespoon of the egg mixture in a cup. Mix the rest into the flour to make dough.

4. Roll out the dough on a floury surface, until it is as thick as your little finger.

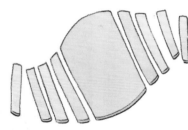

5. Use a blunt knife to cut eight strips as wide as two of your fingers.

6. Bend the strips into wiggles. Pinch the ends. Press one end flat for a head.

7. To make a caterpillar, cut out six circles of dough with a bottle top.

8. Lay the circles in a line. Overlap the edges and press them together.

9. Brush the shapes with the egg mixture. Sprinkle with cheese. Add raisins for eyes.

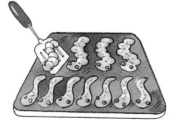

10. Use a fish slice to lift the shapes onto a greased baking tray.

11. Bake for about eight to ten minutes, until they are golden.

    Heat the oven to gas mark 6, 200°C, 400°F

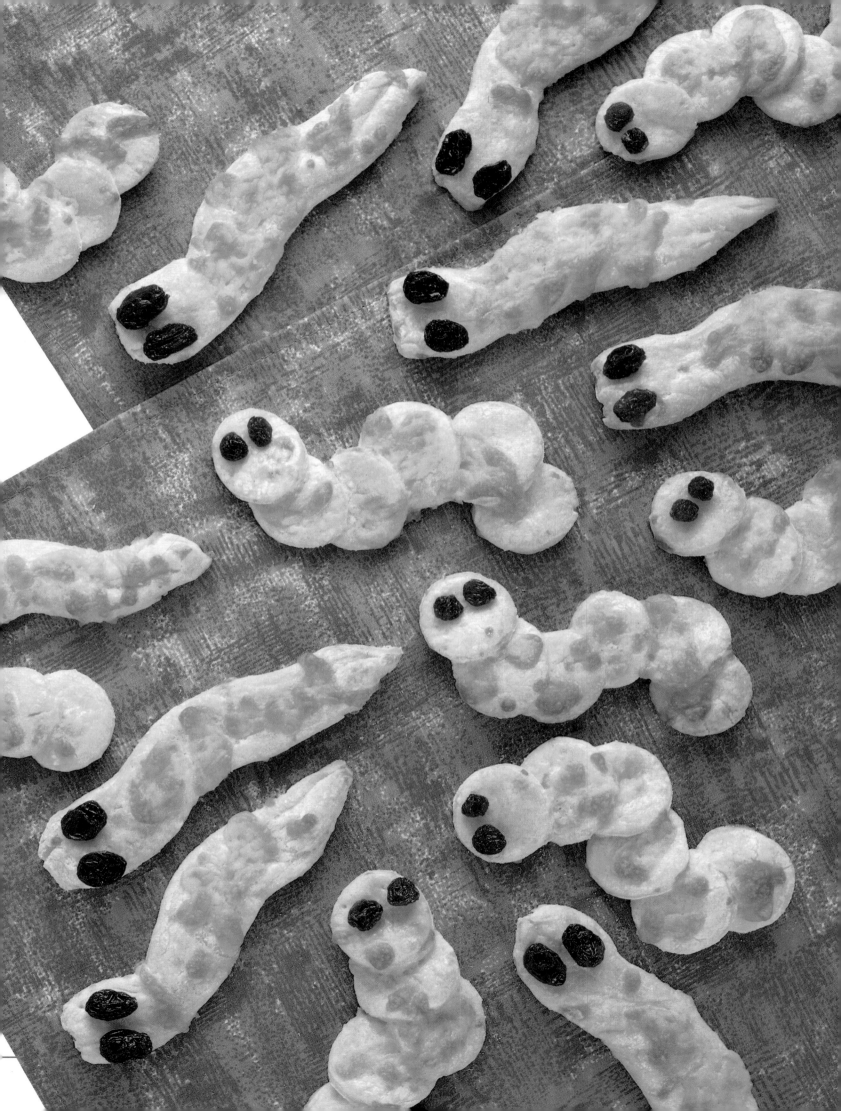

Owl cakes

For ten owls you will need:
225g (8oz) wholemeal flour
½ teaspoon of ground cinnamon
2 level teaspoons of baking powder
75g (3oz) margarine
50g (2oz) demerara sugar
1 medium-sized cooking apple, chopped finely
1 egg, beaten
10 glacé cherries, chopped in half
whole blanched almonds
raisins
greased baking tray

1. Sift the flour, cinnamon and baking powder together in a bowl.

2. Cut the margarine into lumps. Add it to the bowl. Rub it in with your fingers.

3. When the mixture looks like crumbs mix in the sugar, apple and egg.

These owls are delicious if you eat them warm with ice cream.

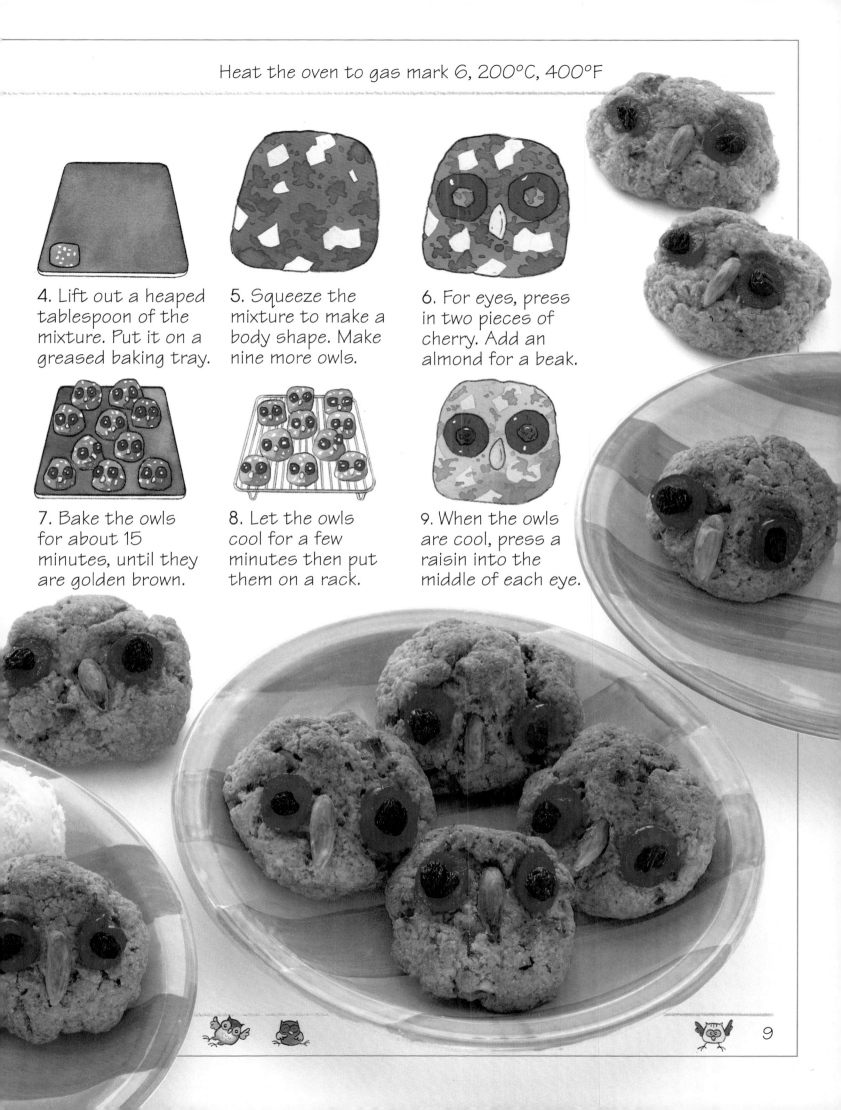

4. Lift out a heaped tablespoon of the mixture. Put it on a greased baking tray.

5. Squeeze the mixture to make a body shape. Make nine more owls.

6. For eyes, press in two pieces of cherry. Add an almond for a beak.

7. Bake the owls for about 15 minutes, until they are golden brown.

8. Let the owls cool for a few minutes then put them on a rack.

9. When the owls are cool, press a raisin into the middle of each eye.

Upside-down pudding

This pudding is made upside-down with the topping at the bottom of the dish. You turn it over once it has cooked.
For the sponge, you will need
100g (4oz) self-raising flour
2 eggs
100g (4oz) caster sugar
100g (4oz) soft margarine

For the topping, you will need:
25g (1oz) butter
400g (14oz) tin of apricot halves, drained
glacé cherries
50g (2oz) brown sugar
20cm (8in) ovenproof dish

For the sponge:

For the topping:

1. Sift the flour into a big bowl. Add the eggs, margarine and caster sugar to the bowl.

2. Stir everything together with a wooden spoon until you get a smooth creamy mixture.

3. Grease the sides of a baking dish. Melt the butter. Pour it all over the bottom.

4. Use your fingers to sprinkle the brown sugar evenly on top of the butter.

5. Put the apricots around the edge, cut-side up. Fill in the middle. Put cherries in the gaps.

6. Spread the sponge over the fruit. Bake on the middle shelf for 45 minutes.

Ice cream goes well with this pudding.

7. Loosen the edges with a knife. Turn the pudding upside-down onto a big plate.

Eat the pudding
while it is still
warm.

You could use thick
slices of cooking apples,
tinned peaches or
pineapple rings.

Turn the oven to gas mark 4, 180°C, 350°F

Shining star biscuits

For about 24 biscuits you will need:
60g (2½oz) soft brown sugar
60g (2½oz) soft margarine
half a small beaten egg
125g (5oz) plain flour
1 teaspoon ground mixed spice
solid boiled sweets
large cutter
small round cutter, slightly bigger than the sweets
a baking tray lined with baking parchment
fat drinking straw

You can use any shape of boiled sweet.

1. Mix the sugar and margarine really well, getting rid of any lumps.

2. Mix in half of the beaten egg, a little at a time. You don't need the other half.

3. Sift in the flour and the spice. Mix it really well with a blunt knife.

4. Squeeze the mixture together with your hands to make a firm dough.

5. Roll out the dough on a floury surface until it is 5mm (¼in) thick.

6. Press out star shapes. Use a fish slice to put them on the baking tray.

7. Make a hole in each star by pressing the straw in one of the points.

8. Use a small cutter to cut out a shape in the middle of each star.

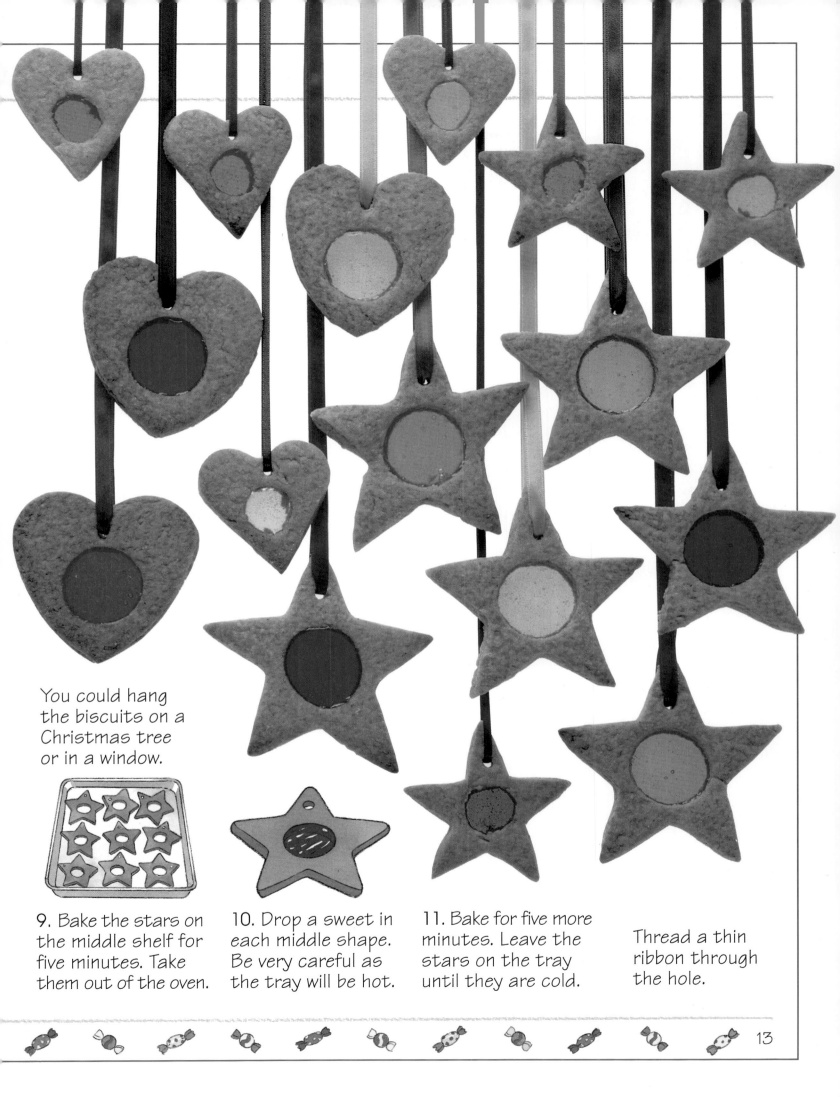

You could hang
the biscuits on a
Christmas tree
or in a window.

9. Bake the stars on
the middle shelf for
five minutes. Take
them out of the oven.

10. Drop a sweet in
each middle shape.
Be very careful as
the tray will be hot.

11. Bake for five more
minutes. Leave the
stars on the tray
until they are cold.

Thread a thin
ribbon through
the hole.

Apricot muffins

For 12 muffins, you will need:
100g (4oz) self-raising flour
50g (2oz) wholemeal flour
1 level teaspoon of baking powder
1 level teaspoon of ground mixed spice
75g (3oz) dried apricots, chopped
110ml (4floz) milk
50g (2oz) butter, melted
1 large egg
2 teaspoons of lemon juice
75g (3oz) soft brown sugar
muffin tin, well oiled

1. Sift the self-raising flour. Add the wholemeal flour and baking powder.

2. Add the spice and apricots. Use a big spoon to mix them in very well.

3. Beat the milk, butter, egg, lemon juice and sugar in another bowl.

4. Use a spoon to make a large hole in the middle of the flour mixture.

You could add glacé cherries, instead of apricots.

5. Pour in half of the beaten mixture. Stir it well. Pour in the rest and mix gently.

6. Put a tablespoon of mix in each hole in the tin. Don't smooth the tops.

You can also make these muffins with chocolate chips, but miss out the spice.

7. Bake for about 20-25 minutes, until the tops are golden brown.

8. Leave the muffins in the tin for five minutes. Put them on a rack to cool.

Flower sweets

You will need:
275g (10oz) icing sugar, sifted
half the white of a small egg, beaten
(or dried egg white,
mix as directed on the packet)
juice of quarter of a lemon
1 teaspoon of peppermint flavouring
yellow and red food dyes
a tray covered in plastic foodwrap
small flower cutter

1. Sift the icing sugar into a deep bowl. Make a hole in the middle of it with a spoon.

2. In a small bowl, mix the egg white, lemon juice and the peppermint. Pour it into the sugar.

3. Use a blunt knife to stir the mixture. Then squeeze it between your fingers until it is smooth.

4. Cut the mixture into three pieces of the same size. Put each piece into a bowl.

5. Put a few drops of red food dye into one of the bowls. Use a metal spoon to mix it well.

6. Put a few drops of yellow food dye into one of the other bowls. Mix it in very well.

7. Sprinkle a little icing sugar on a work surface. Roll the yellow mixture until it is this thick.

8. Use a cutter to cut out as many flowers as you can. Cut them close together.

9. Use a blunt knife to lift the flowers onto a baking tray. Make red flowers in the same way.

10. Pull off a piece of white mixture about this size. Roll it in your hands to make a ball.

11. Press the ball to flatten it a little then press it into the middle of a flower shape.

12. Make lots more white balls and press them into the middles of the flowers.

13. Leave the flowers on the tray for at least an hour until they become hard.

Put some sweets into a box for a present.

Hot bunnies

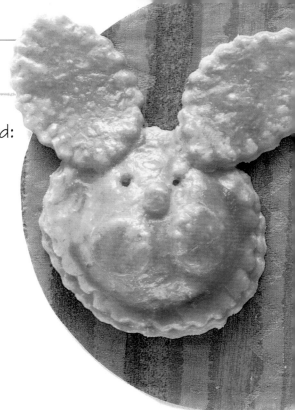

For four bunnies, you will need:
For the pastry:
150g (6oz) plain flour
75g (3oz) margarine
6 teaspoons of very
cold water
pinch of salt

For the fillling:
50g (2oz) sausage meat
1 egg, beaten
large round cutter
bottle top
fat straw
greased baking tray

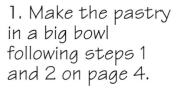

1. Make the pastry in a big bowl following steps 1 and 2 on page 4.

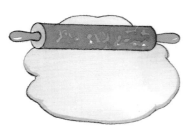

2. Sprinkle some flour onto a work surface. Roll out the pastry thinly.

3. Cut three circles with the cutter and two with the bottle top, for each rabbit.

4. Roll four very small balls of pastry. These will be noses.

5. Use a pastry brush to paint one of the large circles with beaten egg.

6. Put a big teaspoon of sausage meat in the middle.

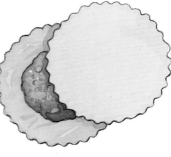

7. Lay one of the big circles on top and flatten it gently with your hand.

8. Press your finger all around the edge to join the circles.

9. Brush the tops with egg. Lift them onto the baking tray with a fish slice.

10. Press on two of the small bottle-top circles for cheeks. Add a nose.

11. Cut one ear by pressing the cutter half way across one of the big circles.

12. Cut another ear from the other side of the of the circle.

13. Press the ears at the top. Brush the ears, nose and cheeks with egg.

14. Make two eyes by pushing the end of the straw into the pastry.

To make a pig, cut out the ears and nose with the bottle top. Cut nostrils with a straw.

15. Bake in the oven for about 15 minutes or until they are golden.

Crown cake

For the cake, you will need:
100g (4oz) soft margarine
100g (4oz) caster sugar
100g (4oz) self-raising flour
2 eggs
20cm (8in) cake tin

For the decoration:
8 cone wafers
ribbon
glacé cherries
bright sweets

For the butter icing:
75g (3oz) soft butter
150g (6oz) icing sugar
lemon juice

To make the cake

1. Mix the sugar and margarine well until the mixture goes creamy.

2. Beat one of the eggs and a little flour into the mixture.

3. Add the other egg and some more flour. Beat them in.

4. Gently mix in the rest of the flour with a metal spoon.

5. Grease the tin. Spoon the mixture in. Bake for about 40-45 minutes.

6. Leave for three to four minutes, then turn the cake out onto a cooling rack.

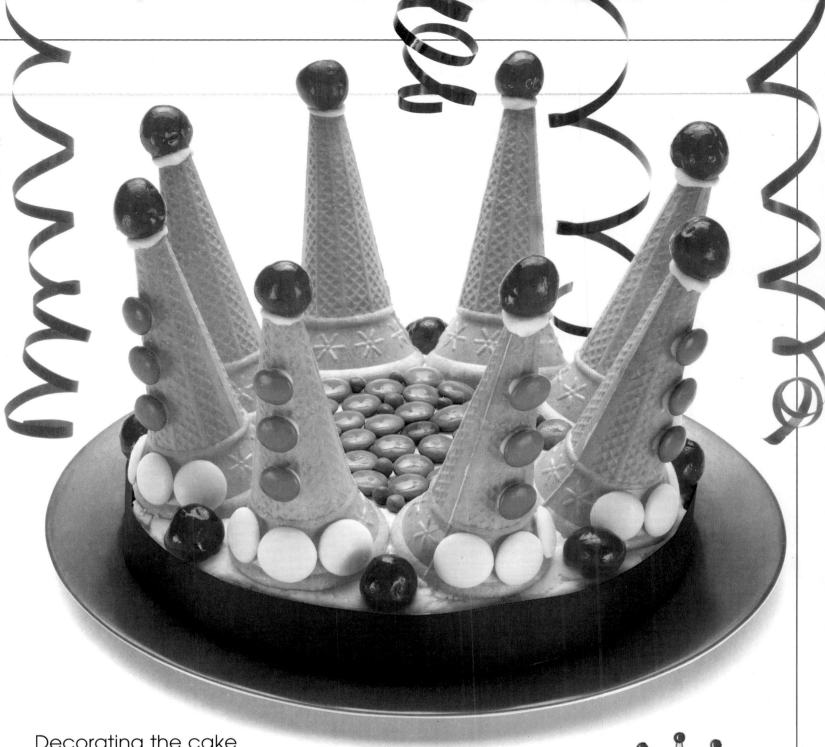

Decorating the cake

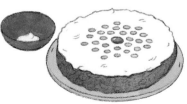

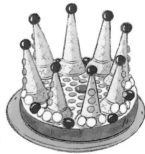

7. Make the icing by mixing the butter and icing sugar. Add a few drops of lemon juice.

8. Put a tablespoon of icing in a bowl. Spread the rest on top. Decorate the middle with sweets.

9. Pinch the ends off the cones. Press them on. Wrap some ribbon around the cake and tape it.

10. Dip the cherries in the spare icing. Press one on each cone. Add more cherries and sweets.

Heat the oven to gas mark 4, 180°C, 350°F

Little cheese tarts

For about 12 tarts, you will need:
150g (6oz) plain flour
75g (3oz) margarine
6 teaspoons of very cold water
pinch of salt
small tin of sweetcorn, drained
50g (2oz) cheese, grated
1 egg
3 tablespoons of milk
round cutter
greased baking tray with shallow pans

1. Make some pastry in a big bowl following steps 1 and 2 on page 4.

2. Sprinkle a little flour onto a work surface. Roll out the pastry thinly.

3. Cut out 12 circles with the cutter. Cut them close together.

4. Grease the baking tray. Press the circles gently into the tray.

5. Put a heaped teaspoon of sweetcorn into each one.

6. Sprinkle some grated cheese on top of the sweetcorn.

7. Beat the egg and the milk in a jug. Pour a little into each tart.

8. Bake them for 15-20 minutes until they are golden and puffy.

9. Lift the tarts onto a rack and leave them for a little while to cool.

You can eat the tarts when they are either warm or cold.

Heat the oven to gas mark 5, 190°C, 375 °F

Painted biscuits

To make about 20 biscuits you will need:
50g (2oz) icing sugar, sifted
75g (3oz) soft margarine
the yolk from a large egg
vanilla essence
150g (6oz) plain flour, sifted
cutters
greased baking tray

To decorate the biscuits:
beaten egg yolk
food dyes

1. Mix the icing sugar and the margarine until they are smooth.

2. Mix in the egg yolk, stirring it well. Add a few drops of vanilla essence.

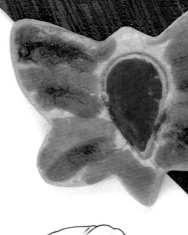

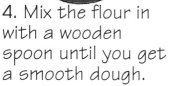

3. Hold a sieve over the bowl and pour in the flour. Shake it through the sieve.

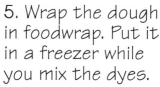

4. Mix the flour in with a wooden spoon until you get a smooth dough.

5. Wrap the dough in foodwrap. Put it in a freezer while you mix the dyes.

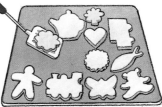

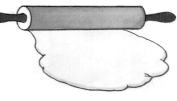

6. Put some egg yolk onto saucers. Mix a few drops of food dye with each.

7. Roll out half the dough quite thinly on a floury surface. Then roll the rest.

8. Use big cutters to press out shapes. Cut them close together.

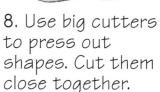

9. Use a fish slice to lift the biscuits carefully onto a baking tray.

10. Press lightly with small cutters to make patterns on the biscuits.

11. Use a very clean paintbrush to paint shapes with the dyes.

12. Bake them for 10-12 minutes. Let them cool a little. Put them on a rack.

Decorate your biscuits with lots of different patterns.

This makes lots of biscuits so you could freeze some of the dough to use another day.

Coconut mice

For eight large mice, three medium mice, three
baby mice and eight pieces of cheese, you will need:
250g (10oz) icing sugar
200g (8oz) tin of condensed milk
175g (7oz) desiccated coconut
red and yellow food dyes
red liquorice 'bootlaces' or thick yarn
silver cake decorating balls
sweets for ears

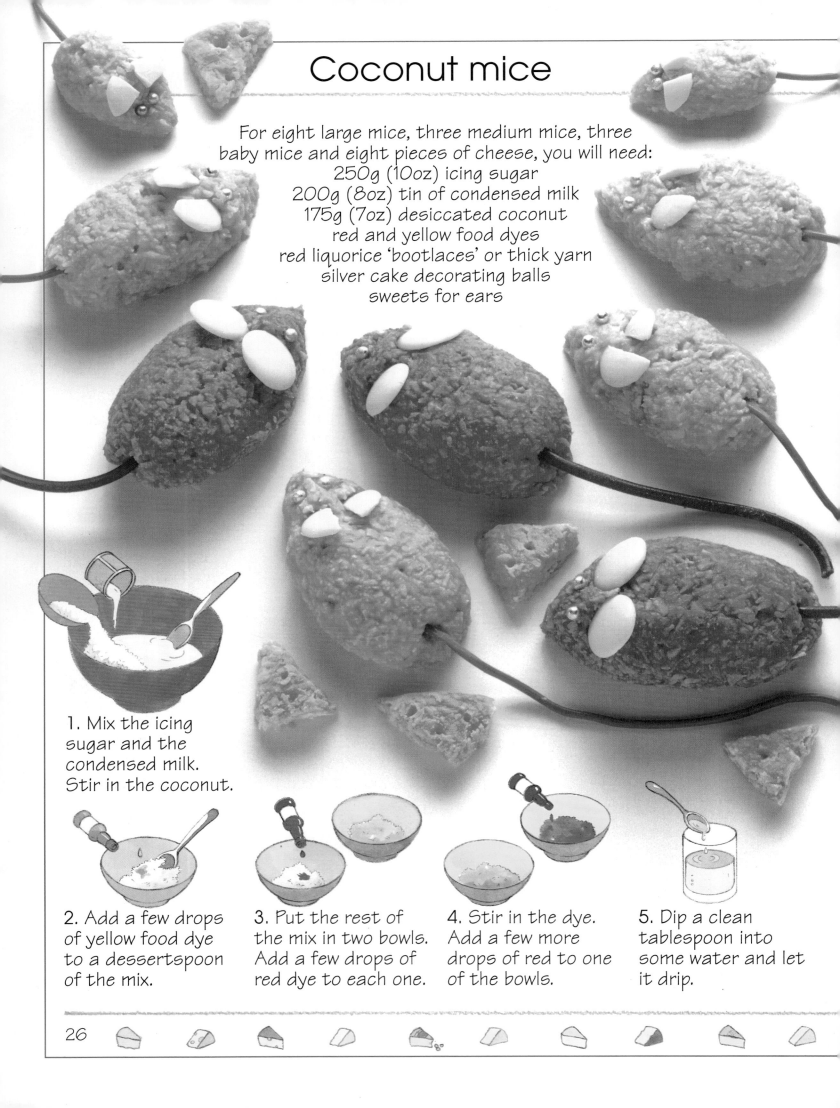

1. Mix the icing
sugar and the
condensed milk.
Stir in the coconut.

2. Add a few drops
of yellow food dye
to a dessertspoon
of the mix.

3. Put the rest of
the mix in two bowls.
Add a few drops of
red dye to each one.

4. Stir in the dye.
Add a few more
drops of red to one
of the bowls.

5. Dip a clean
tablespoon into
some water and let
it drip.

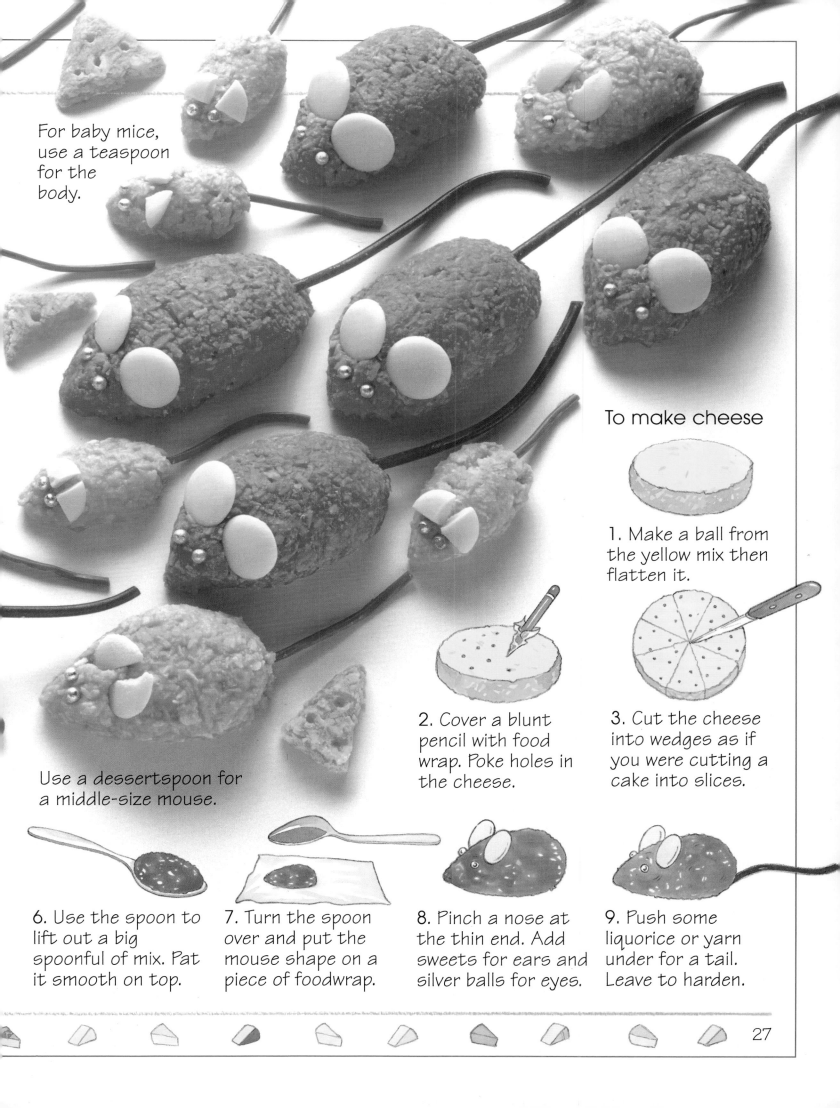

For baby mice, use a teaspoon for the body.

Use a dessertspoon for a middle-size mouse.

To make cheese

1. Make a ball from the yellow mix then flatten it.

2. Cover a blunt pencil with food wrap. Poke holes in the cheese.

3. Cut the cheese into wedges as if you were cutting a cake into slices.

6. Use the spoon to lift out a big spoonful of mix. Pat it smooth on top.

7. Turn the spoon over and put the mouse shape on a piece of foodwrap.

8. Pinch a nose at the thin end. Add sweets for ears and silver balls for eyes.

9. Push some liquorice or yarn under for a tail. Leave to harden.

Easy pizza

Cheese and sweetcorn

For one 25cm (10in) pizza you will need:
225g (8oz) plain flour
½ teaspoon of salt
2 tablespoons of oil
150ml (¼pt) of milk
75g (3oz) cheese, grated
4 tomatoes, thinly sliced
a pinch of mixed dried herbs

Topping ideas:
sliced mushrooms
sweetcorn
(tinned or frozen)
pineapple
chopped ham
pepperoni

1. Sift the flour and salt together in a big bowl. Make a hole in the middle with a spoon.

2. Mix the milk with the oil in a jug. Mix it well. Pour it carefully into the hole in the flour.

Pepperoni, mushroom and cheese

Heat the oven to gas mark 6, 200°C, 400°F

3. Use a blunt knife to stir the mixture well, until it makes a sticky dough.

4. Sprinkle a little flour onto a work surface. Roll the dough into a circle as wide as this page.

6. Add more toppings if you want. Bake on the top shelf for 15-20 minutes.

5. Cover the dough with the sliced tomatoes. Sprinkle the cheese on top. Add the herbs.

Chopped ham, cheese and tomato

Sweetcorn, cheese and pineapple

Christmas tree cakes

For about 15 cakes, you will need:
100g (4oz) self-raising flour
100g (4oz) soft margarine
100g (4oz) sugar
2 eggs
paper cake cases
baking tray with shallow pans
assorted sweets

For the butter icing:
50g (2oz) butter or margarine, softened
100g (4oz) icing sugar, sifted
food dye
squeeze of lemon juice or a few drops of
vanilla essence

1. Follow steps 1 and 2 on page 10 to make a sponge mixture.

2. Put the cases in a baking tray. Half-fill each one with sponge mixture.

3. Bake them for about 20 minutes. Leave them on a rack to cool.

4. To make the butter icing, stir the butter until it is creamy.

5. Add some of the icing sugar. Stir it in. Mix in the rest, a little at a time.

6. Stir in a few drops of food dye and the lemon juice or vanilla.

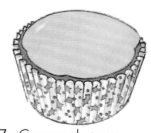

7. Spread some icing on top of each cake. Put a sweet in the middle.

8. Put small sweets around the middle one to make a pattern.

  Heat the oven to gas mark 5, 190°C, 375°F

Use bright sweets to make different patterns on your cakes.

31

Sunshine toast

You will need:
1 slice of bread
margarine
1 medium or small egg
large cutter
baking tray

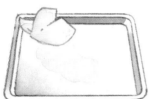

1. Dip a piece of kitchen paper into some margarine and rub it all over a baking tray.

2. Spread margarine on one side of the bread. Press the cutter hard in the middle of the bread.

3. Lift out the shape you have cut. Lay the pieces of bread on the tray, with the butter up.

4. Break the egg onto a saucer. Carefully slide the egg into the hole you have cut.

5. Bake for seven minutes on the top shelf of an oven, or for a little longer if you don't like a runny yolk.

6. Lift the pieces of bread carefully off the tray. Eat it while it is warm.

 Heat the oven to gas mark 6, 200°C, 400°F

What shall I be?

Contents

A circus strongman

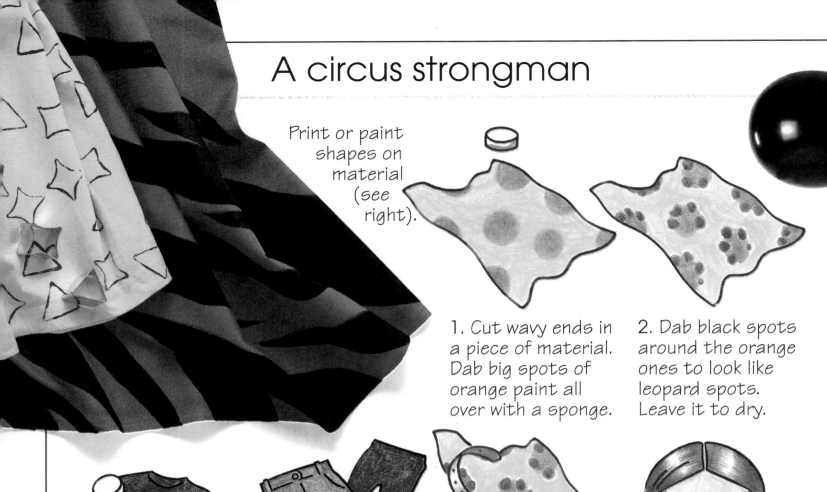

Print or paint shapes on material (see right).

1. Cut wavy ends in a piece of material. Dab big spots of orange paint all over with a sponge.

2. Dab black spots around the orange ones to look like leopard spots. Leave it to dry.

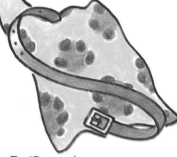

3. Tape a sponge to the top of each of your arms. Pull on a long-sleeved T-shirt over the top.

4. Pull on a pair of bright tights then put on a pair of dark shorts on top of them.

5. Put the spotty material over one shoulder. Fasten it around your waist with a belt.

6. Put some hair gel in your hair. Part your hair in the middle and smooth it down.

Make some weights

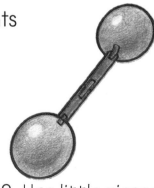

7. Dip a damp sponge in red face paint. Dab it lightly over your cheeks.

8. Use a brush and dark face paint to to draw big eyebrows. Add a curly moustache.

1. Blow up two balloons. Paint two tubes from the middle of kitchen paper towels.

2. Use little pieces of tape to join the tubes together. Tape a balloon on at each end.

Print shapes on a bright vest with paint and a cookie cutter.

Face paint a hairy chest.

A scarecrow

1. Tape lots of clean dry straw or long grass inside an old hat.

2. Sponge brown face paint in patches on your face. Sponge red on your cheeks.

3. Brush on spikey eyebrows and a moustache with brown face paint.

4. Dab face paint on your nose and add big freckles. Brush red on your lips too.

5. Pull on a big checked shirt and some old trousers or a skirt.

6. Put on some old boots or shoes. Put elastic bands around your ankles.

7. Put elastic bands around your wrists. Don't make them tight.

8. Push straw into your cuffs and trouser legs, under the elastic bands.

Tie a bright scarf around your neck and pin a toy mouse to your hat.

Put a belt around your tummy and push straw under it.

A snow queen

Make a crown

  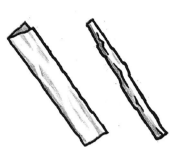 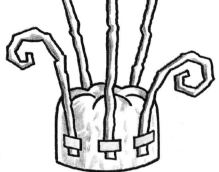

1. Spread glue inside the bottom part of a big plastic bottle. Press pieces of foil onto it.

2. Cut out four pieces of foil as big as this book. Cut each piece in two from end to end.

3. Fold each piece of foil in half like this. Squeeze each one into a long, thin shape.

4. Tape five of the pieces evenly around the bottom of the crown. Curl the ends over.

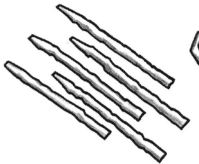   

5. Cut the other pieces of foil in half. Pinch one end to make pointed icicles.

6. Tape five of the icicles around the bottle in between the long ones. There will be one icicle left.

7. Cut some foil as long as this book. Fold it over and over. Tape it around the bottom of the crown.

8. Wrap the spare icicle around one of your fingers for a ring. Twist the end into a spiral shape.

Snowflakes

 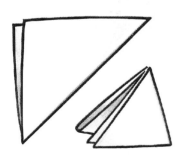 

A wand

1. Cut a small square of thin white or silver paper.

2. Fold the square diagonally to make a triangle. Fold it in half again.

3. Cut different shapes along each edge then open it out and flatten it.

Cover a thin garden cane in foil. Glue a snowflake to one end of it.

See pages 62-63 to paint your face like this.

Press some self-adhesive stars onto your hair.

Use an old skirt or piece of material for a cloak. Glue or pin on some snowflakes and stars.

Attach the crown to your hair with hairgrips.

Fasten the cloak with a brooch.

39

A puppy

1. If your hair is short, tie a ribbon or a piece of elastic around your head.

3. Tuck the socks into the band. Use hairgrips to hold them in place.

2. Stuff a pair of short socks with lots of cotton wool balls.

4. Dab white face paint over your face. Close your eyes when you get near them.

Long hair

1. If your hair is long, tie it into two high bunches.

2. Push each bunch into a short sock. Fasten them with bands.

5. Dab orange face paint on in patches. Brush black on the end of your nose.

7. Brush a black line from your nose to your top lip. Brush along your lip too.

6. Use a brush and brown face paint to add spots and big patches.

8. Add a red tongue on your bottom lip. Add dots either side of your nose.

After you have painted your face, put socks on your hands and feet, for paws.

41

A lucky pirate

1. Sponge light brown face paint over your face.

2. Brush on big eyebrows and a curly moustache.

3. Dab stubble on your chin with a toothbrush.

4. Cut out an eyepatch shape from stiff black paper.

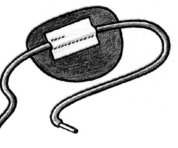

5. Tape a bootlace across the back of the eyepatch, near to the top.

6. Get someone to tie the eyepatch and knot a scarf around your head.

7. Slip an elastic band through a curtain ring. Hang it over your ear.

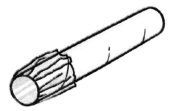

8. For a telescope, paint a cardboard tube. Put foodwrap over one end.

Use face paint to make a scar on your cheek.

Put some old necklaces and brooches in your treasure box too.

Make a treasure box

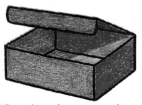

Find a box with a lid, like a chocolate or teabag box. Paint it.

Cover things like bottle tops and biscuits with foil to make treasure.

Face paint
a curly
beard
instead
of stubble.

You could safety pin
a toy parrot on your
shoulder.

Wear a
leather belt
across one
shoulder.

A doctor

1. For a doctor's coat, use an old white shirt. Cut the sleeves to fit.

2. Push the lenses out of old sunglasses. Wear the frames.

3. For medicine, fill plastic bottles with water. Add a few drops of food dye.

4. Use a pillow for a bed. Fold a pillowcase in half for a top sheet.

Make a stethoscope

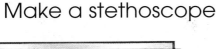

1. Cut a piece of foil twice as long as this book. Fold it in half.

2. Fold the foil in half again then scrunch it up tightly.

3. Fold the foil in half. Pull the two ends apart and bend them in.

Use a lunch box for a doctor's case.

Make bandages from strips of material.

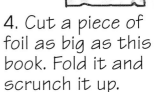

4. Cut a piece of foil as big as this book. Fold it and scrunch it up.

5. Bend one end around the long piece. Tape a jar lid on the other end.

Make a thermometer

Cut a strip of foil. Wrap it around the end of a straw and tape it on.

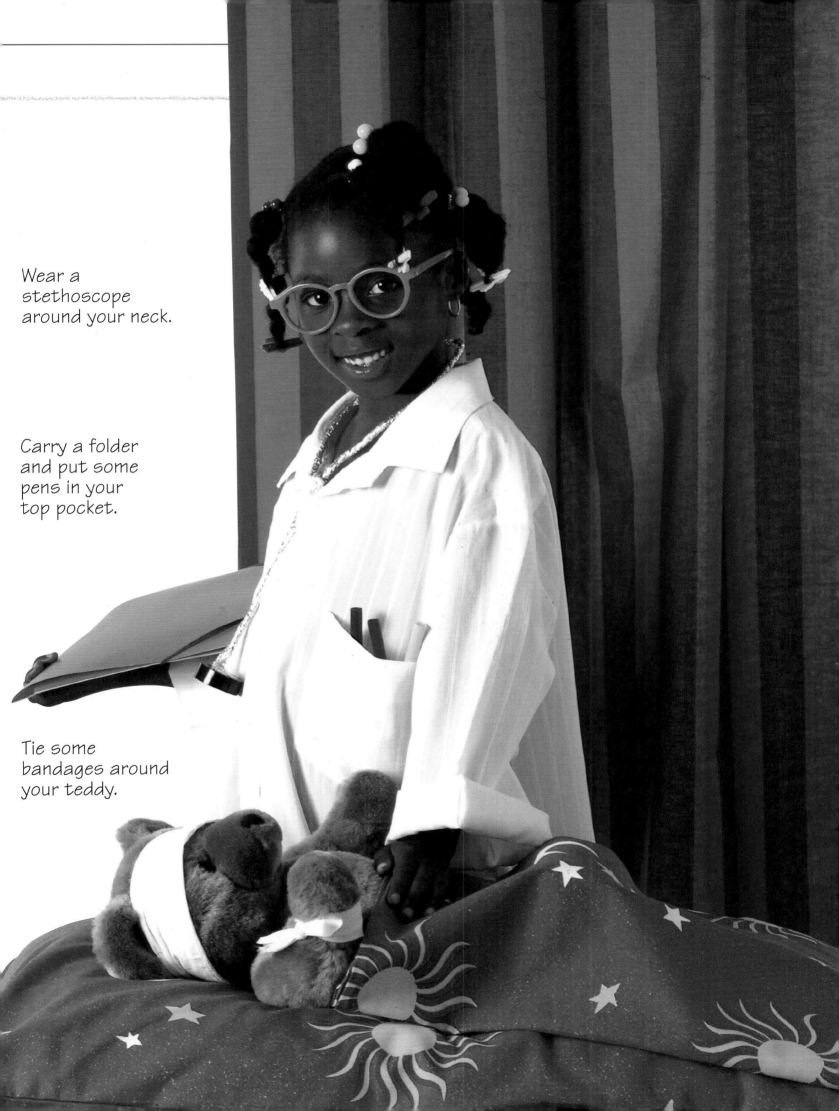

Wear a stethoscope around your neck.

Carry a folder and put some pens in your top pocket.

Tie some bandages around your teddy.

A spotted bug

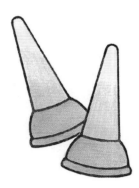   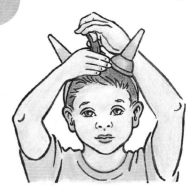

1. Put two ice-cream cones on newspaper. Paint them then leave them to dry.

2. Cut a strip of thin cardboard to fit over the top of your head. Glue the cones onto it.

3. Bend the cardboard around your head. Fasten it at each side with hairgrips.

4. Put a blob of hair gel onto your hand. Lift up a big clump of your hair in your other hand.

Remember you can't eat the cones once they are painted.

5. Squeeze your gelled hand around a clump of hair and pull it up. Do this to more clumps of hair.

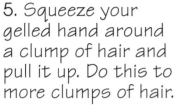

Put face paint on your hands and arms.

6. Rub a damp sponge in face paint. Dab it over your face. Leave gaps for spots.

7. Use a brush and a different face paint to draw the outlines of spots in the gaps.

8. Fill in the spots with a brush. Close your eye when you fill in any spots that are near it.

Cut out spots and tape them onto a bright T-shirt.

A rich lady

Make some bank notes

1. Cut four pieces of newspaper as big as this book. Fold them in half like this.

2. Fold the top edge down to the bottom. Then fold the top down to the bottom again.

3. Open out each piece of paper. Cut carefully along all the lines you have folded.

4. Write numbers on each piece of paper with a felt-tip pen. Keep them in a handbag.

Carry lots of bright shiny things in a handbag.

5. Pull on a bright T-shirt and a long floaty skirt. Put a belt around your waist.

6. Put on bright lipstick. Dab some pink powder or face paint on your cheeks.

7. Put on several necklaces, brooches and some big earrings. Wear a watch.

Carry a toy dog. Tie a belt around its neck for a lead.

Put on some sunglasses.

Wear a long scarf around your shoulders for a shawl.

8. Wrap a ribbon around a big hat. Use a safety pin to attach some big flowers on the side.

9. Scrunch up some paper and push it into the toes of a pair of high-heeled shoes.

10. Put on the shoes and the hat. Put on some gloves and wear lots of rings on top of them.

Carry a handbag.

A funny clown

1. Sponge white all over your face. Draw red circles on your cheeks and nose.

2. Brush a big smiley shape around your mouth and fill it in.

3. Brush two arch shapes over your eyes and fill them in carefully.

4. Carefully draw black lines across your eyes. Add thin eyebrows.

Wear a bright T-shirt. Cut buttons from felt or paper and tape or glue them on.

Wear trousers that are too big for you. Use safety pins to attach ribbons, for braces.

Make a clown hat

1. Cut a roll of bright crêpe paper as wide as this book.

2. Cut the paper in two. Make cuts nearly to the top of each piece.

3. Tape the uncut edges inside a big hat. Tape them on at the sides.

4. Shake the hat to fluff out the hair. Tape on a fake flower at one side.

Big bow tie

1. Cut a piece of crêpe paper the same size as this book.

2. Fold it in half, long sides together. Put an elastic band around the middle.

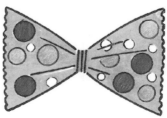

3. Stretch out the two ends. Press on self-adhesive or gummed shapes.

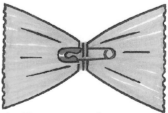

4. Put a safety pin through the elastic band and fasten it onto your clothes.

A chef on television

Make a chef's hat

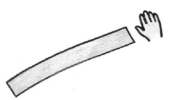

1. Cut a strip of white cardboard as tall as your hand and which fits around your head.

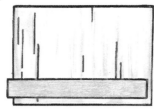

2. Cut a piece of white crêpe paper so it is the same length as the cardboard.

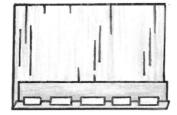

3. Lay the cardboard near the bottom of the paper. Fold the bottom edge over and tape it in place.

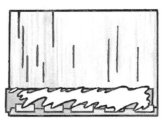

4. Put glue on the cardboard. Fold the cardboard over onto the crêpe paper and press it flat.

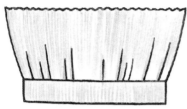

5. Hold the paper at each side. Pull your hands apart gently to stretch the paper like this.

6. Bend the cardboard around your head. Use small pieces of tape to join the ends.

7. Gather the top edge of the paper together and wrap an elastic band around it.

8. Press down the top of your hat so that it is flat on top. Puff it out around the sides.

Joke sausages

1. Carefully cut one leg from an old pair of pink or brown tights.

2. Squeeze four sheets of toilet paper to make a sausage shape.

3. Roll four pieces of paper around the sausage. Push it into the tights.

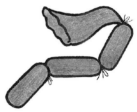

4. Tie thread at the end of the sausage. Make more sausages the same way.

Dressing up

Brush on a moustache with face paint. Add a little beard.

Put on an apron. Dip your fingers in flour and dab them over the apron.

Act as if you are doing a television show about cooking.

Dab some flour on your nose.

Collect some bowls, pans and spoons from your kitchen. Put them on a table in front of you.

53

Cinderella

Before

Pull some wispy bits from cotton wool and put it in your hair, as cobwebs.

1. Cut the bottom of an old skirt into rags. Sew or use safety pins to add bright patches.

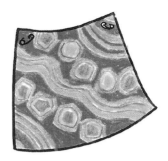

2. Use a safety pin to fasten a piece of bright material around your waist as an apron.

3. Fold a scarf like this. Wrap it around your shoulders and knot the ends in front of you.

4. Sponge some pink face paint on your cheeks. Add some grey for dirty patches.

Make a broom

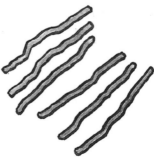

1. Collect lots of thin twigs. Snap them so that they are all about the same length.

2. Make them into a bunch around a garden cane. Wrap string around and around then tie it.

After

1. Pull on some pale tights and put on a pretty vest, leotard or swimsuit.

2. Tie some elastic around your waist. Tuck a piece of net curtain into it for a skirt.

3. Tie a strip of material or a piece of ribbon around your waist to hide the elastic.

4. For gloves, cut half way down the legs of some old lacy tights. Cut the toes off too.

Paint your face

1. Dip a paintbrush in red face paint. Brush red flowers on your forehead and on your cheeks.

2. Brush a bow near each eyebrow and wavy lines between the flowers. Add green leaves too.

Make a pretty fan (see page 57).

Tie bows on your shoulders and in your hair.

Glue fake flowers to your skirt.

Cinderella's sisters

Make a wig

1. Cut a piece of cotton wool roll as wide as this page. Then cut it into eight pieces.

2. Twist each piece to make ringlets. Clip them to your hair in front of your ears.

3. Cut another piece of cotton wool and clip it over your head to cover your hair.

4. Pull the cotton wool a little to make it lumpy. Glue on a big bright bow from a parcel.

Paint your face

1. Sponge pale pink face paint all over your face. Make your cheeks a darker pink.

2. Brush on long eyelashes. Put on some very bright lipstick and add a beauty spot.

For a bright wig, dab paint on the cotton wool and let it dry before you put it on.

Make a fan

1. Cut a piece of gift wrap so that it is as wide as this book and twice as long.

2. Fold over one of the short edges. Turn the gift wrap over then fold the edge up again.

3. Keep folding the gift wrap over and over in this way until you get to the end of it.

4. Wrap some tape around it at the bottom. Snip shapes out at the top. Open it out.

Instead of a wig, make two plaits from wool. Use hairgrips to clip them to your hair.

Tie a scarf around your head to hide the ends of the plaits.

Long nails

Cut ten pointy shapes from sticky paper. Lick them and press them over your own nails.

Put on some necklaces and rings.

57

A long-armed giant

1. Scrunch up paper and push it into a pair of rubber gloves to make them stiff.

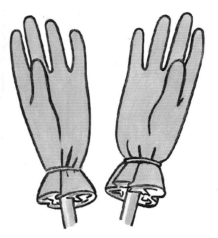

2. Push the round ends of two wooden spoons inside. Fix them with elastic bands.

3. Push a cushion up under your T-shirt to make a very fat tummy.

4. Put a big sweater over your T-shirt. Fasten a belt around your waist.

5. Dip a damp sponge in red face paint and dab it on your nose and cheeks.

6. Wet a brush and dip it into dark face paint. Draw on bushy eyebrows.

7. Face paint wiggly shapes across your chin to make a curly beard.

8. Add dark freckles across your nose and paint white teeth on your bottom lip.

9. Pull your cuffs over the ends of the gloves. Fasten them with elastic bands.

Wear big boots and a waistcoat.

Hold the handles of the spoons when you move your arms.

A very old person

1. Brush your hair back. Use a sponge to stroke grey or white face paint over your hair.

2. Dip the sponge in pale pink or white face paint and dab it all over your face.

3. Dab dark pink over your cheeks. Then dab some brown down each side of your nose.

4. Use a brush and brown face paint to add some thin lines across your forehead.

5. Brush two thin brown lines at the top of your nose, between your eyebrows.

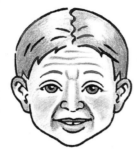

6. Add a line from each side of your nose to your mouth. Smudge the lines with your finger.

7. Dip a toothbrush in grey and dab it on your face for stubble, or put on bright lipstick.

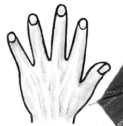

8. Brush thin blue or white lines on the back of your hands.

Collect some things like these to wear or carry.

For glasses, get someone to help you to take the lenses out of an old pair of sunglasses.

Wrap a scarf around your neck and wear a hat.

Painting your face

You can use face painting crayons, but the face paints which look like a box of paints are the best to use.

1. Make sure that your face is clean and dry. Put on the dressing-up clothes you are going to wear.

2. Wrap a towel around your neck to protect your clothes. Tie your hair back or put on a hairband.

3. To cover your face in face paint, dip a sponge in water then squeeze it until no more water comes out.

4. Rub the sponge around and around in the face paint. Dab it all over your face, right up to your hair.

5. Close each eye and dab over your eyelids very carefully. Press the sponge over your lips too.

Scarecrow
- page 36

Cinderella
- page 54

6. Wash your sponge and dip it into a different shade of face paint. Dab it lightly all over your cheeks.

7. Gently rub a thin wet paintbrush around in a face paint. Draw on eyebrows with the tip of the brush.

8. Use a thin paintbrush to add very fine lines on your forehead, around your eyes and on your cheeks.

9. Use a paintbrush to add glitter face paint. Press little stars into it. They will stick as the paint dries.

10. Use face paint on your lips too. Brush around the shape of your lips then fill them in.

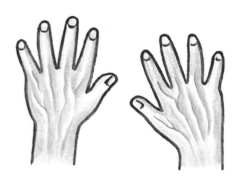

11. You can also put face paint on your hands and arms. Use a sponge to dab it on. Add lines with a brush.

Giant
- page 58

Clown
- page 50

Things you need

You will need face paints for most of the projects.

Strongman
yellow material
a belt
a long-sleeved T-shirt
two small sponges
coloured tights
a pair of shorts
hair gel
two balloons
two cardboard tubes
tape

Scarecrow
clean, dry straw or
    long grass
an old hat
old trousers or a skirt
checked shirt
old boots or shoes
elastic bands

Snow queen
3 litre plastic bottle
kitchen foil
white or silver paper
a thin garden cane

Puppy
3 pairs of short socks
cotton balls
a ribbon or elastic
    (if your hair
    is short)
hairgrips
mittens

Pirate
stiff black paper
a bootlace
a bright scarf

Pirate: continued
a curtain ring
elastic band
a small box
things for treasure
a cardboard tube
plastic foodwrap

Doctor
an old white shirt
old sunglasses
plastic bottles
food dye
pillow and two pillowcases
kitchen foil
a jar lid
a straw

Spotted bug
two ice-cream cones
a strip of cardboard
paint
hairgrips
hair gel

Rich lady
a bright T-shirt
a long skirt
jewellery
a handbag
lipstick
face powder
newspaper

Funny clown
crêpe paper
big bright hat
self-adhesive or gummed
    shapes
a safety pin

A television chef
white cardboard
white crêpe paper
toilet paper
old brown or pink tights
thread
flour
striped apron

Cinderella
an old skirt
scraps of material
a big scarf
a brooch
thin twigs
a garden cane
pale tights
a vest, leotard or swimsuit
elastic and ribbon
a net curtain

Cinderella's sisters
cotton wool roll
hairgrips
bright parcel bow
gift wrap
sticky paper
old lacy tights

Long-armed giant
a pair of rubber gloves
two wooden spoons
a cushion
a belt
a big sweater
elastic bands

Very old person
old sunglasses
hat and scarf

With thanks to Ben Bokaie, Raz Budeiri, Inigo Choong,
Kezia Evans, Pippa Green, Jessica Hopf, James Jacob, Martha Kiff,
Kattja Madrell, Emma Pearson, William Rowlands,
Kyrie Simon-Penfold and Yasmin Wilson

What shall I grow?

Contents

Green-haired creatures

1. Wet an old sock and put it into a mug. Turn the top over the rim.

2. Use a spoon to spread lots of grass seeds all over the bottom.

3. Use an old spoon to fill the mug with potting compost.

4. Wrap an elastic band tightly around the sock. Chop off the top.

5. Pour water onto the top of the sock. Lift it up and let it drip.

6. Turn it upside down. Put it on a saucer and pour water around.

7. For a nose, carefully push a pin through one of the holes in a button.

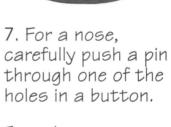

To make a hedgehog, squash the sock into a pointy shape.

8. For eyes, push in some more pins with buttons near the nose.

9. Put your creature into a warm, light room. Make sure you keep the top wet.

You can cut the 'hair' short and let it grow again.

A giant sunflower

1. You need to buy a packet of sunflower seeds. Put stones into the bottom of a small pot.

2. Fill the pot with potting compost. Press in two seeds. Leave a gap between them.

3. Water your pot. Put it outside in a light place. Water it often to stop it from drying out.

4. Two seedlings should grow. Pull out the smaller one so that the other one grows well.

5. When the plant is about as high as your hand, get help to plant it in a bigger pot.

6. Water your plant and leave in a light sunny spot, which is out of the wind.

7. When your plant is as high as your knee, push a cane into the compost. Tie the stem on.

8. As the plant grows taller, carefully tie its stem to the cane higher up.

Look on the seed packet to see how tall your flower might grow.

9. When the petals fall from the flower, leave the seeds on the plant to grow and ripen.

10. Shake out a few seeds from the head to plant next year. Leave the rest for the birds to eat.

Sunflowers have huge flowers and can grow very tall.

Plant your seeds in the spring.

Your plants will
grow flowers
in summer.

A tiny garden

Use small plants such as pansies, primula, ivy, trailing lobelia and alyssum.

1. Get someone to help you to make holes in the bottom of an old plastic washing-up bowl.

2. Cover the bottom of the bowl with small pebbles or pieces of broken pots.

3. Use a small spade to fill the bowl almost to the top with potting compost.

4. For a pond, make a hole in the compost. Put a shallow plastic carton into it.

5. Put small pebbles into the bottom of the carton. Fill it with water.

6. Cut a lawn from a piece of turf. Put it beside the pond and water it well.

7. Dig small holes and plant a mixture of small plants around your lawn and pond.

8. Put some plastic dolls' house furniture onto the lawn. Add a tiny cat or dog too.

Plant this at any time.

Cress shapes

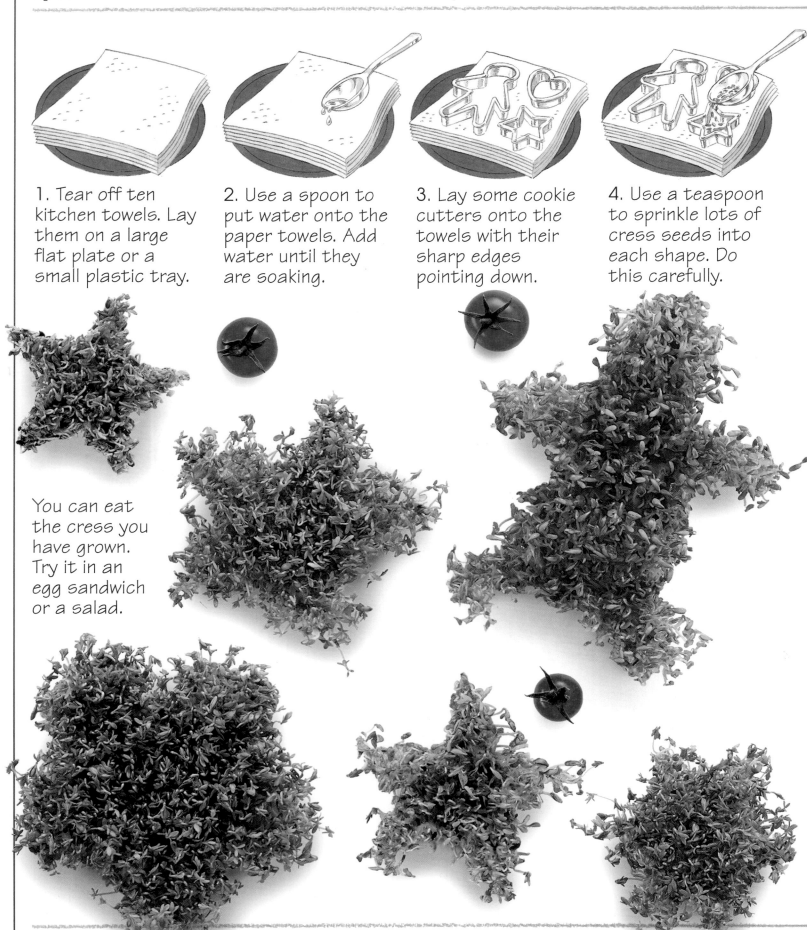

1. Tear off ten kitchen towels. Lay them on a large flat plate or a small plastic tray.

2. Use a spoon to put water onto the paper towels. Add water until they are soaking.

3. Lay some cookie cutters onto the towels with their sharp edges pointing down.

4. Use a teaspoon to sprinkle lots of cress seeds into each shape. Do this carefully.

You can eat the cress you have grown. Try it in an egg sandwich or a salad.

You can grow these at any time. They will grow in four to five days.

5. Spread the seeds all over each shape with your fingers. Hold the cutter as you do it.

6. Lift the cutters off the towel leaving the seed shapes. Put them in a light place.

7. Use a spoon to water around the seeds every day. Don't put water on the seeds.

8. When the cress is as long as your little finger, cut it off so you can eat it.

Tiny islands in the sea

1. Cut the top off some vegetables which have sprouted a little. Cut them as thick as this.

Use vegetables such as carrots, parsnips, turnips and beetroot.

2. Put a little cold water into a shallow dish. Spread the vegetable tops over the bottom.

3. Carefully pour in a little more water around the vegetable tops but don't cover them.

4. Put the dish on a windowsill. Add a little water each day. The shoots will grow in a few days.

Your shoots should grow to look like tall trees on islands.

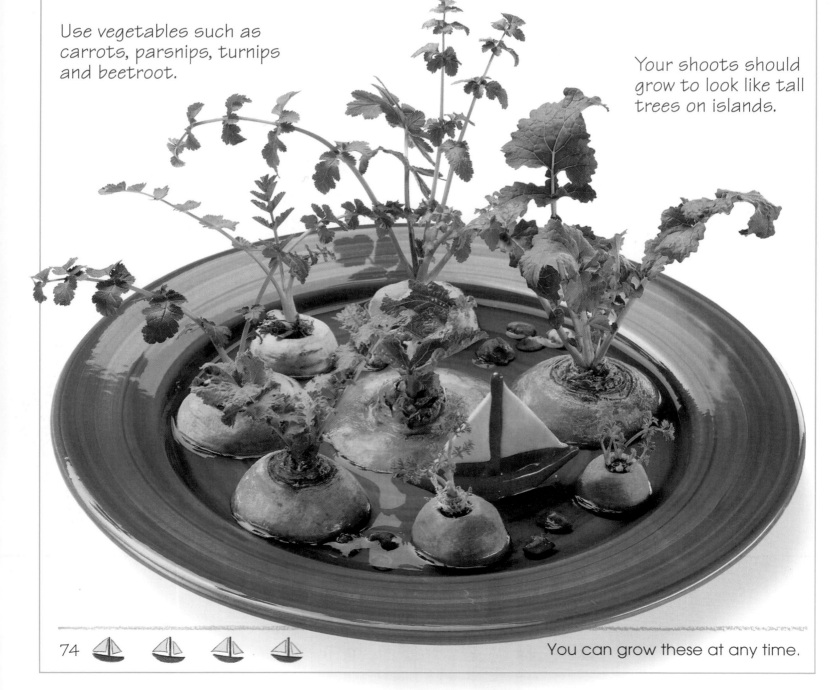

You can grow these at any time.

A spiky plant

1. Cut the top off a pineapple so that the yellow part of it is as thick as this.

2. Lay it on its side on a plate. Leave it on a windowsill for two days so that it dries out a little.

3. Fill a pot with compost. Put the pineapple top on top. Press more compost around.

4. Water it and leave it in a warm place. New leaves will grow in the middle.

Water your pineapple plant often.

Grow when you can buy a ripe pineapple.

Crocuses in a silver pot

1. Turn a pot upside down and lay some kitchen foil over it. Make a hole in the top of the foil.

2. Turn the pot over. Press the edges of the foil inside the top of the pot.

3. Use a spoon to put potting compost into the pot. Fill it about halfway up.

4. Put some crocus corms (which look like bulbs) into the pot with their pointed ends up.

5. Fill the pot almost to the top with more compost. Water it so that it is damp.

6. Put the pot into a cool, dark place. Look at it once a week. Water it if it feels dry.

7. When the shoots are as long as your thumb put the pot into a light, cool place. Keep it damp.

8. When the shoots grow taller, put the pot in a light place. The flowers will come out.

Cut shapes from paper and glue them on the foil.

Plant in the autumn to bloom in the spring.
They take 10 to 12 weeks to grow.

When the flowers die, cut the heads off. Plant the corms in your garden and they may flower again next year.

Stand your pot on a saucer to stop it marking surfaces.

Try planting miniature daffodil bulbs in the same way.

Potatoes in a bucket

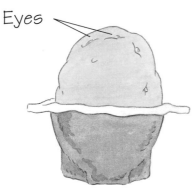

Eyes

1. Put a potato into an eggbox, with its eyes at the top. Leave it for several weeks until it grows shoots.

2. When the shoots are as long as this, rub off most of the shoots but leave two which look strong.

3. Make holes in the bottom of an old bucket. Cover the bottom with stones then add some potting compost.

4. Push the potato into the compost with the shoots pointing up. Cover it with compost. Leave it outside.

5. In about four weeks, you'll see some shoots. Cover them with compost and water your bucket.

6. Add more compost and water it every time the shoots appear. Do this until the bucket is full.

7. After a while, flowers will grow. Water your plant often. If a potato appears, cover it with some compost.

8. After four months the plant will die. Tip the compost out. See how many potatoes have grown.

Don't forget to water your plant if the compost feels dry.

Keep your potatoes in a cool, dark place until you are ready to cook and eat them.

Pots of pansies

1. Rinse the bottom part of an eggbox under the tap. Let it drip.

2. Put some potting compost in the sections. Don't fill them to the top.

3. Put two pansy seeds into each section. Leave a gap between them.

4. Sprinkle some more compost on top of the seeds and press it down.

5. Cover the eggbox with a newspaper and leave it outside in a cool place.

6. Keep the seeds moist. After about two weeks, shoots will begin to show.

7. Take off the newspaper so that the shoots can get plenty of light.

8. When they have grown two leaves, pull out the smaller shoot.

9. As your pansies grow, roots will grow through the sides of the eggbox.

10. Soak the eggbox and gently pull the sections apart.

11. Half-fill a pot with compost. Put one section into it. Add more compost.

12. Put your pots outside on warm days, but bring them in at night.

You can plant your pansies straight into the garden if you like.

Paint your pots with acrylic paint if you like.

Roots and shoots

1. Soak a big jar and peel off its labels. Soak three broad bean seeds in a saucer.

2. Rinse the inside of the jar with cold water. Empty it out but don't dry it.

3. Fold a paper napkin in half. Curl it into a circle and slip it inside the jar.

4. Press the napkin against the side of the jar with the handle of a spoon.

5. Peel back part of the napkin. Push a broad bean seed in against the jar.

You can grow these at any time. They take two to three weeks.

6. Add the other beans around the jar. Wet the napkin with lots of water.

7. Put the jar in a bright, warm place. Add water often to keep the napkin wet.

Leafy stems

1. You need a pot or a mug and some florist's foam (the kind used to arrange flowers in a vase).

2. Soak the foam in a bowl of water. Leave it in the water until bubbles stop coming to the surface.

3. Push the foam into your pot. Use scissors to trim it so that it is a little bit below the top of the pot.

4. Ask if you can cut pieces from plants which have woody stems. Make them just longer than your hand.

5. The pieces you have cut are called cuttings. Snip a straight end just below a leaf of each cutting.

6. Pull off the bottom leaves. Push the end of the stem into the foam near to the edge.

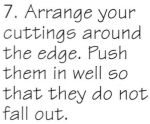

7. Arrange your cuttings around the edge. Push them in well so that they do not fall out.

8. Put your pot on a windowsill but out of very bright sunshine. Water the foam often to keep it damp.

9. When new leaves grow, take the foam out of the pot and look and see if roots have grown.

10. Take a blunt knife and carefully cut the foam away from each cutting. Try not to damage their roots.

11. Plant each cutting in a pot full of potting compost. Water it and put it outside in a warm, light place.

Do this in autumn. They will grow in 6-8 weeks.

When you plant your cuttings, make sure that don't forget to water them.

Cuttings in foam.

Rosemary

Box

Sage

You can plant more than one ivy cutting in a pot.

Lavender

Ivy

Bean sprouts to eat

1. Put two large spoons of mung beans into a sieve. Rinse them.

2. Soak the beans overnight in cold water. They will swell a little.

3. Lay some cotton wool roll in a plastic tray. Put water on it to make it damp.

Eat your mung beans in a crunchy salad.

4. Put two egg cups upside down onto the tray. Spread the beans all over.

5. Slide the tray into a foodbag. Then put it in a black bin bag. Put it in a very warm, dark place.

6. Check each day that the cotton wool has not dried out. Water it to keep it damp.

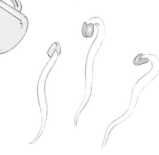

7. When the shoots are this long, pull them off the cotton wool. Rinse them well.

    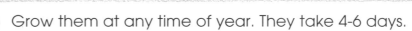

Tasty tomatoes

1. You will need to buy two or three small tomato plants. Get them from a garden centre.

2. For each plant, put stones into a big plant pot. Cover them with potting compost.

3. Gently tip each plant out of its pot. Put one in each big pot. Try not to squash the leaves.

4. Add more compost to fill the pot. Gently press the compost around each plant.

5. Water your plants well and leave them outside in a sunny place. Bring them in if it is frosty.

6. Water your plants every day, especially if it is hot and sunny. Flowers will grow.

7. As your plants grow taller, carefully push a cane into the pot and tie the stem to it.

8. After the flowers have died, little tomatoes will grow. Pick them when they turn red.

Plant them in spring and you'll get tomatoes in summer.

A leaf into a plant

1. Fill a small bottle with water. Don't fill it quite to the top so that you leave a small space.

2. Cut a paper square and fasten it over the top of the bottle with an elastic band.

3. Use scissors to cut off a leaf with its stalk from an African violet.

4. The leaf should be from near the outside and should look healthy.

Leave your plant in a light place, but not on a very sunny windowsill.

Grow at any time.

5. Hold the bottle. Make a hole in the middle of the paper with a very sharp pencil.

6. Push the stalk through the hole. Its end should go in the water. Add more water if you need to.

7. When tiny roots grow and new leaves appear it is ready to plant in a pot.

8. Make a hole in some compost. Put the plant in it and gently press around it. Water your plant.

Put your pot on a saucer. When you water it, put the water in the saucer, not on the plant.

Herbs on your windowsill

1. Buy some fresh herbs which are growing in a pot from a supermarket.

2. Wash out some empty half litre (one pint) milk cartons. You will need one for each herb.

3. Dry the cartons. Snip halfway down one side. Then cut the top off all the way around.

4. Turn each carton over. Make a hole in the bottom with the point of a sharp pencil.

5. Put some stones into the bottom of each carton. Spoon in a little potting compost.

6. Take each herb out of its pot by tipping it over and tapping the bottom of the pot.

Dill

Chives

7. Fill the gap between the carton and the roots with compost. Press the top of the compost.

8. Cut a strip of paper long enough to go around and slightly wider than each carton.

9. Wrap one of the pieces of paper around each carton. Tape it at the back.

10. Put your herbs onto a tray and leave them on a windowsill. Keep the compost moist.

Parsley

Basil

Thyme

A sweet-smelling flower

Grow a hyacinth in soil

1. Use an old spoon to put potting compost into a pot. Don't fill it to the top.

2. Gently press the bulb in the middle, with the bud on top. Add more compost.

3. Stand the pot on a saucer. Carefully water around the bulb.

4. Put it in a cool, dark place for eight to ten weeks. Keep the compost damp.

5. When it has grown as high as your first finger, put it in a light, cool place.

6. When it grows a little taller, put it in a warm place. A flower will grow.

Grow a hyacinth in water

1. Cut two foil circles and lay them over a tumbler. Press the bulb on top.

2. Carefully press the foil down all around the sides of the tumbler.

3. Lift off the bulb. Make a 2.5cm (1in) slit in the middle of the foil.

Elastic band

4. Snip the slit to make a cross. Fill the tumbler with water, up to the foil.

5. Sit the bulb on top of the cross. Leave it in a cool, dark place.

6. When the roots have grown long, move your bulb into a cool, light room.

Plant several bulbs together in a bowl, but don't let them touch.

This is a special glass you can buy for growing a hyacinth.

An ivy tower

1. Put stones into a very large pot which has a hole in it. Fill it with potting compost.

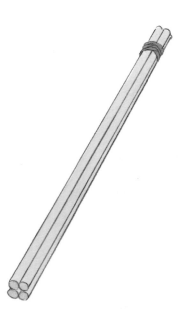

2. Use an elastic band to fasten four short garden canes together near to one end, like this.

3. Spread out the canes. Push them well into the pot, with their ends nearly touching the sides.

4. Dig a small hole at the bottom of one of the canes. Put an ivy plant into the hole.

5. Add a little compost around the plant and press it down firmly with your knuckles.

6. Dig a hole at the bottom of the other three canes. Plant an ivy in each hole.

7. Hold the longest stem of each plant and twist it carefully around its cane. Water your plants.

8. As the ivy grows, twist each stem around its cane every two or three days.

Paint your pot with acrylic paint and put lots of Christmas decorations on your ivy tower.

A moss garden

1. Put a thin layer of potting compost into the bottom of a shallow tray, with no holes in the bottom of it.

2. Hunt for some moss on lawns, walls and between paving slabs. Look on stones and pieces of bark too.

3. Dig up small pieces of moss and put them on your tray. Add mossy stones and pieces of bark.

4. Collect some rainwater if you can, but tap water will do, and spray or sprinkle the moss well every day.

Watch your mosses grow.

Add some shells too.

Grow at any time.

First published in 1998 by Usborne Publishing Ltd, 83-85 Saffron Hill, London EC1N 8RT, England.